PUBLISHED by PARABLES
Earthly Stories with a Heavenly Meaning

Pathways To The Past

Each volume stands alone as an Individual Book
Each volume stands together with others
to enhance the value of your collection

Build your Personal, Pastoral or Church Library
Pathways To The Past contains an ever-expanding list of
Christendom's most influential authors

Augustine of Hippo
Athanasius
E. M. Bounds
John Bunyan
Robert Lewis Darby
Brother Lawrence
Jessie Penn-Lewis
Bernard of Clairvaux
Andrew Murray
Watchman Nee
Arthur W. Pink
Thomas Watson
Hannah Whitall Smith
R. A. Torrey
A. W. Tozer
Jean-Pierre de Caussade
And many, many more.

The Providence of God

By
Richard Sibbes

The Providence of God
Richard Sibbes

Published By Parables
November, 2019

All Rights Reserved. No part of this book may be reproduced or utilized in any form or by any means, electronic or mechanical, including photocopying, recording, or by any information storage and retrieval system, without permission in writing from the author.

ISBN 978-1-951497-39-2
Printed in the United States of America

Readers should be aware that Internet Web sites offered as citations and/or sources for further information may have been changed or disappeared between the time this was written and the time it is read.

The Providence of God

By
Richard Sibbes

But I trust in the Lord that I myself also shall come shortly.—PHIL. 2:24.

IN the former verses the apostle Paul shews his care and love that he bore to the Philippians, in that he would not leave them destitute of a guide and director; and therefore he sends Timothy, whom he commends, to shew his love the more; and for his greater commendations, he shews the wickedness of the contrary sort, that thereby Timothy his sincerity may the better appear; 'others seek their own, but Timothy as a son hath served me.' He lays down the causes of this his sincerity. He first had learned the Scriptures of a child; then he had a gracious grandmother and mother. It is an excellent comfortable thing whenas children can say, 'I am the son of thy servant and thy handmaid,' Ps. 86:16. And a third cause or help was his conversing with him. He drew in the sweet spirit of the blessed apostle. God, he derives† good to men by good society. They are therefore enemies to themselves that regard not good, choice company; for it makes of good excellent, and of those that are not yet good, if they belong to God, it makes them good.

In this verse he shews a further degree of his care of the Philippians. There are‡ divers ways to come to the knowledge of men's estate; as first by report; secondly, by messengers; thirdly, by letter. St Paul had used all these; but his care was such as all these would not content him. He must see them himself, which is indeed the surest means and way of all.

In these words, therefore, consider the manner of the delivery of this speech, 'I trust in the Lord.' Then the matter, which contains a purpose of his coming. Then the ground, his trust in God. Here, first of all, mark the language of Canaan; and the heavenly dialect,

1. To express future purposes with a reservation of, and resignation to, God's will and guidance. 'I trust in God,' saith the apostle; for the hearts of men, yea of kings, are in God's hand, to turn and wind them as the rivers of waters, Prov. 21:1. This shews Christ to be God, for he is the object of trust. Observe in the second place,

2. God's providence extends to every particular thing. He guides our incomings and our outgoings; he disposes of our journeys; nay, his providence extends to the smallest things, to the sparrows and to the hair of our heads; he governs every particular passage of our lives.

Use 1. This should teach us to set upon our affairs with looking up to heaven for permission, power, and sufferance; and this St James enforces by reproving the contrary. 'Go to,' saith he in his fourth chapter, and ver. 13th, and adds the instruction thereupon; 'for that ye ought to say, if the Lord will, we shall live and do this or that.' Let us therefore in all our affairs be holy, and not bind or limit our holiness only to coming to church; but seeing at all times and in all places we are Christians, and ever in the presence of God, let us place ourselves still in his eye, and do nothing but that we would be willing God shall see; and labour to behold him in every good thing we have, and give him thanks in all the good we enjoy.

Use 2. And secondly, it ought to give us warning, that we ought not to set upon anything, wherein we cannot expect God's guidance: and so consequently cannot trust on him for a blessing upon what we do. For if we do, we must look to meet the Lord standing in our way, as Balaam did, in opposing our lewd and wicked intentions.

Use 3. And thirdly, it ought to teach us to take nothing but that for which we may give God the thanks and praise; as contrarily many do, who may thank the devil for what they have gotten, and yet make God implicitly the giver of their most unjust exactions.

VERSE 25

Yet I supposed it necessary to send to you Epaphroditus.

Paul thought it not enough to plant the seeds of the word amongst them, but he would be viewing it and watering. 'I purpose shortly to see you,' saith he; but because I am now in prison I cannot come myself, but I purpose presently to send you Epaphroditus, and afterwards Timothy; and this he thought necessary—for well he knew that the residence of the pastor is necessary to the flock of the Lord, in some sort. But to stand upon this doctrine is not my purpose. The next thing I come to is, the commendations of Epaphroditus, which is divers; out of which generally thus much we learn, that it is our duty to give them commendations that are praiseworthy, even to this end that thereby we might raise a good opinion of them, especially of the ministers of the gospel; for hereby is the gospel itself glorified by us. And indeed it is a great sign that the spirit of the devil rests in that man, that doth detract and disparage the good children of God. For it comes hereby that the gospel of God is also blamed, and neglected. For the commendation of the minister is a preparative, and makes way for the word.

My brother

The word in this place signifies one of the same office. As judges call one another 'brother,' so doth St Paul call Epaphroditus 'brother,' in regard of his office and spiritual function; and hereby he shews his love to him; for 'brother' is a name of love and friendship. Secondly, it shews his care of Epaphroditus; for one brother will care for another, unless they be of a Cainish nature. Thirdly, it is a name of equality, for brothers are equal. And hereby the apostle shews his humility, who being an apostle and pillar of the church, descended so low as to call one of inferior rank and calling, 'brother.' He had another spirit before his conversion; he persecutes the church of God. But afterward those that he formerly persecutes are now his 'brethren.' Now he thinks he is a debtor to all, both Jew and Grecian, Rom. 1:14. The proud man thinks all are debtors to him, that all do owe him respect and reverence; and indeed it is the spirit of the devil that 'lifteth up.' Antichrist is his eldest son indeed, who lifteth himself up against, and above all that is called God. Contrarily Christ humbles himself to the death to call us brothers. Shall we then disdain to live together in terms of equality and love? Is there not infinite difference between Christ and us? Was there not in him such a glory as passeth our apprehension? and what had we, or what have we, that we should lift ourselves up after this fashion? If we will strive to be above and outgo others, let it be in humility. Go each before others, in giving honour to others above ourselves. Observe, therefore, grace takes advantage of all bonds to increase love; bonds of office as well as of nature. Men of the same profession emulate and envy one another. Thus it is naturally, but let religion teach us better, and take away this natural poison from us.

Fellow-labourer

The apostle commends him yet further. He calls Epaphroditus his 'fellow labourer,' in regard of the pains he endured; and 'fellow soldier,' in regard of the perils and dangers he jointly did undergo with the apostle. The doctrine that hence arises is, that ministers are fellow-labourers. They are not, or should not be, fellow-loiterers, as many are. No. The Scriptures compares them to the most painful and laborious professions; to husbandmen, whose labour is circular, every year renewing as the year doth renew. Such is the ministers' labour, converting and strengthening others. It is a great labour to break the shell of the word; to lay open the right interpretation thereof; to divide it aright; to convert a soul; to preserve it from the devil. It is as the peril of women in travail; 'My little children, of whom I travail in birth till Christ be formed in you,' saith Paul our apostle in Gal. 4:19. Idle people are therefore unjust esteemers and judgers of the pains of ministers, they knowing it is out of their proper element.

Use. If ministers then be labourers, you to whom we preach are God's orchard; you must submit yourselves to be wrought on. If we be builders, you must be lively stones of this building. You must suffer yourselves to be squared, and cut, and made fit for this building while you are here. At the building and finishing of the material temple there was no noise of hammers, or such instruments; all were fitted in the mountain. Thus* must we expect to be fitted here while we live; for in that beautiful temple in heaven, there is no fashioning or fitting, either by crosses to hammer us, or by any other means. We must here be conformable to his death, that we may also be conformed to the similitude of his resurrection hereafter. If ministers be husbandmen, you must be 'ground,' and such as may bring forth fruit to perfection, else all our labour and pains that we take with you will be to no other end than to make you to be near cursing, Heb. 6:7. And know, it is not sufficient that you bring not forth evil fruit; but every tree that bringeth not forth good fruit, must be hewed down and cast into the fire, Mat. 3:10. Remember Christ cursed the fig-tree for unfruitfulness; and with what curse? Even unfruitfulness. Thus will God do with us. If he finds us unfruitful, he will take away his Spirit, and we shall be unfruitful still;

and this† by woeful experience we see daily, with many that come indeed within the sound of the word every day, but mend not one jot; nay, they become every day worse. May not God complain, as he did of Judah in the parable of the vineyard, Isa. 5:5, that he hath hedged us and fenced us about with government, and authority, and good laws, and hath taken out of us the stones and thorns of popery, and profaneness; and yet we bring forth wild grapes. And might he not break down the wall; and that justly, and suffer us to be devoured. Surely yes; and yet must needs we acknowledge him to be just. But it follows, the apostle calls Epaphroditus here his,

Fellow-labourer. It is observable here, concerning God's goodness, that he suffers not his faithful labourers to be alone. Christ sends them out by 'two and two,' before his face, Mark 6:7; and this he doth that they might be a mutual aid, strengthening and comforting one another. Thus did Christ in old time, and thus he doth also in later times. He sent Augustine and Jerome, Luther and Melancthon; where, by the way also, observe God's wisdom in sending men of diversity of gifts: Jerome, severe and powerful; Augustine, meek and gentle; Luther, hot and fiery; Melancthon, of a soft and mild spirit; one to temper the other's over forwardness, and thereby to prevail with some that liked not of the strictness of the other. And by this means God sent teachers suitable to the natures and fitting the several humours of men, among whom some desire to hear the 'sons of consolation,' others the 'sons of thunder.'

Fellow-soldier

Every man's life is a warfare, but most of all and above all, the minister is continually in war and strife. They are soldiers, leaders; they carry the standard, but they of all others are in the most danger, they stand in the brunt of the battle. The reason hereof is: the devil, having malice against the whole church in general, specially aimeth at them that pull men out of his service into the church, even as beasts do rage against such as take their young away from them. It is the minister that treads on the serpent's head: no marvel, then, if the devil endeavoureth to bite them by the heel. Thus dealt he with Christ, when he first set upon his office of mediator; and thus did he with Moses and Paul, in the main plots contrived against them. Such as those are great eyesores to him, and this is it that makes them soldiers and captains. But how? I answer, even as Paul, 1 Cor. 10:4. So the ministers do fight against the strongholds of corruption within us, against natural reason, corrupt affections, proud conceits; they fight against these imaginations, and in them, against the devil himself, who doth* use these instruments to bring his purposes to pass.

In ministers, therefore, it is required principally knowledge in the stratagems of the devil, in especial manner in those amongst whom they should converse; by observing the corruptions of the times, places, and the corrupt customs, and also the general corruptions of callings. He, therefore, that would be a good soldier, had need be continually resident in his charge; for the devil having gotten hold once, he seeks to sing them asleep with 'Soul, thou hast much goods,' &c., Luke 12:19. This is dangerous. The minister had need look to it; for men do soothe themselves up in pleasure, thinking that religion may well stand with the love of the world. The watchman must tell them plainly, 'You cannot serve God and mammon.' If these false conceits, this false divinity that is in us, were once removed, we should easily resist the devil. Our enemies are within us, and therefore what saith Christ? 'The prince of this world cometh, and hath found nothing in me,' John 14:30, and therefore he got nothing. 'Be not deceived,' saith St Paul; thereby shewing that their offence did arise of a false conceit and an error in judgment. If then the ministers be soldiers under Jesus Christ our general,

Use 1. Then all by nature are in an opposite kingdom. We have natural lusts in us against every commandment, and there is no act of faith in us, but we have false conclusions in us to fight against them. We are by nature not only void of all goodness, but we have a nature opposite to all goodness.

Use 2. The second use is for instruction. If we would be brought and redeemed out of this estate, let us not hold forth against the ministry of the gospel. Some will have such carnal conceits, that do what we can, they will not see; they are wilfully blind. Such as these are by the ministry of the gospel hastened to hell. Their course is made more swift, their fall more desperate. Let it not be with us so; but let us come with yielding hearts to the word, not resisting the Spirit. God will not always strive with us, but will give us up to our own courses, to live and die under the dominion of the devil, and so will glorify himself in our confusion. For the word is as the man on the white horse which is spoken of in the Revelation, it goes forth conquering, it condemns men already, Rev. 19:11. It is like Jonathan's bow, it never returns empty from the blood of the slain,* 2 Sam. 1:22. Christ he continues to preach to us here by his Spirit, as he did to those in the time of Noah, 1 Pet. 3:19. If we will not hear, we shall into prison, as they are now without redemption, for blood shall be upon our own heads.

Use 3. In the third place, if ministers be soldiers for us, let us help them by our prayers. 'Curse Meroz,' saith the angel of the Lord. Why? 'Because they came not to help the Lord,' Judges 5:23. If those are cursed with a bitter curse, that came not to help them that fight for the Lord, what curse remaineth to them that fight against them, and deprave them that fight for the Lord?

Use 4. Lastly, Seeing we are here in a working estate, nay, in a warring estate, it should make us more willing, nay, to desire, to be dissolved, and to be with Christ, where all assaults and trials shall cease, all tears shall be wiped away. And therefore, if we see afflictions, be not terrified, for God will give thee strength here and hereafter. Thou shalt be recompensed in the resurrection of the just.

But your messenger, and he that ministered to my wants

The word in the original that is translated 'messenger,' signifieth an apostle,† and it may be taken, either for a messenger sent by them to the apostle Paul, or for a messenger sent by the apostle Paul to them. However, it is an honourable office to be an ambassador to the church of God, or to be a messenger from the church of God; and therefore the Philippians sent him that was most dear to them to the apostle Paul, out of the love they bare to him; and Paul again would not keep him long from them, because he loved them. It is a happy contention, when men contend who shall express most love and affection toward each other. This Epaphroditus brought refreshing to the apostle, being then in durance, from the Philippians. Whence observe,

Doct. 1. That the child of God is subject to wants here whiles he lives. Thus it is with them at all times. Thus is it with us. Sometimes we want this thing, sometimes that; but [he] gives them what they most want. Thus was it with Christ. He wants water, and was constrained to beg it of a poor silly woman, John 4:7, seq. And if it was thus with Christ, we must not look for better. And therefore, let us be comforted against it; for, as it followeth in the next place,

Doct. 2. The children of God shall be satisfied. Rather than Elias shall perish for hunger, the ravens shall feed him, 1 Kings 17:4.*. If rich Dives will not have mercy on such, the brutish dogs shall, Luke 16:21. For Paul, God provides one Epaphroditus, or Onesiphorus, 2 Tim. 1:16–18. In Acts 16:25, Paul's trials were many; but see, those places which of themselves were places of horror become† so comfortable as in them he sings psalms; and those persons that were his tormentors, become his great friends and comforters in his adversities. So that assuredly, one way or other, God will provide for his children, especially for his ministers. And therefore Christ bids his apostles, that when they went to preach, they should not carry anything with them; for well he knew that those that were converted would not suffer them to lack anything that was necessary. It must encourage us to our work. God, he will give us wages, even for the performance of our ordinary duties of our callings, if we do them in obedience to his laws. And indeed, if we could live by faith as we should, we would not care for anything, for God hath promised liberally, and if we could believe, he would not be less than his word, who doth suffer his children to want some few outward things, but it is for their good. And to such God ever gives patience to suffer, and to expect and wait the time of God's visitation.

VERSE 26

For he longed after you all.

Epaphroditus, he longed after all the Philippians; yea, there was none but he had a regard of; yea, of the meanest, whom he knew to be as dear in Christ's acceptation as the greatest. For the soul and salvation of the meanest cost him as dear as the salvation of the greatest. Again, the weakest are soonest discontented and most subject thereunto, who therefore ordinarily are soonest brought to complain. It is a ground therefore for the ministers so to behave themselves, that they also have a respect unto all the meanest even as the greatest.

And was full of heaviness

It grieved Epaphroditus to think that they mourned for his sickness. Grief returns by reflection on the party loved. Observe then the wicked nature of men that make music in the sorrow of others. Surely they have a poisonous heart within them; and it ought to reprove those that regard not to grieve those by whom they were brought into the world. Surely if such had the principles of nature within them, such a slavish condition of serving their own unbridled lusts could never settle on them.

Because that ye had heard that he had been sick. For indeed he was sick, &c.

Observe here how one wave follows another. After Epaphroditus had endured a long and dangerous voyage, he meets with a long and dangerous sickness. It is the nature of us. Let us not dream of any immunity. God's children are subject to sicknesses while they live. Daily experience proves it; for they have bodies that have the seeds of sickness in them. Their heaven is not here; for they are not clean from corruption, which bringeth death and sickness, by which also God intends good to the body. For if such recover, their bodies are purged from many bad humours; if they do not recover it, God by little and little unties the marriage knot between the soul and the body, and so death comes more easy. And thus also grace is strengthened in the soul; as the outward man is weakened, so is the inward man renewed, 2 Cor. 4:16. For by sickness we are put in mind to make even our accounts with God, and by it he also makes pleasures of the world to be bitter unto us, that we may the more willingly part with them; even as nurses use to anoint the pap with some bitter thing to make the child refuse the pap. Observe in the second place, that God often suffers his children to come to extremities, yea, even to death itself, and into desperate estates. Thus did he suffer Hezekiah, Job, Jonas, David, Daniel, and the 'three children' to run into the jaws of death. Thus suffered he also his disciples to be overwhelmed with water ere he would seem to take notice of it.* Nay, thus suffered he his only Son Christ upon the cross while he said, 'My God, my God, why hast thou forsaken me?' and by this means it comes to pass that when all natural and ordinary means fail them, their trust is not placed on the means, but on some more durable and constant help, upon God's own good will and power. For else our nature is such as soon we should idolise the means, and set them in the place of God, if means should continually recover us. And this offence was Asa† guilty of in his sickness; he trusted not the Lord, but physicians. God is jealous of our affections. And hence lest Paul should be lifted up, he gave him over to some base temptation, which he calls 'the messenger of Satan.' In the second place, God suffers his children to fall into extremities, to the end that we having experience of God's helping hand in them, we might come to rely more confidently on him in all adversities. He suffers us to receive the sentence of death in us, to the end that we should not trust in ourselves, but in God, 2 Cor. 1:9. For God is never nearer than in extremities. His power is seen in man's weakness. In the third place, God suffers us to fall into extremities that he might try what is in us, and that he might exercise the graces in us. And commonly it is seen, those that rely upon means in such extremities make themselves executioners of themselves. Thus did Saul, Ahithophel, and Judas; for while they trust on the means, they failing them, what marvel if they seeing no remedy run into despair, whenas God's children go to their own Father, exercising their faith, hope, prayers, and all Christian graces and duties. And therefore afflictions are called trials, because they try our graces. For if it were not for them, we should not know what faith, patience, hope, or grace were. Fourthly, hence it comes that the communion between God and us might be more sincere; for whenas nothing is between God and us to rely on, then do we come more sensibly and experimentally to taste, see, and feel God more to our comfort; for where ordinary helps fail, God's help begins.

The use of all this is, That we should not be dismayed, though we be in the most forlorn estate; for in extremity God is most near us, and then shall our graces be strengthened, and we shall have experience of God's favour strengthening us. And in the second place, when thou seest any in great afflictions, pronounce not thy sentence rashly on him, for even then he may be nearest God: Ps. 41:1, 'Blessed,' saith the prophet, 'is he that considereth the poor aright: the Lord will deliver him in the time of trouble.' The papists, indeed, are unmerciful in this kind. See what he is by his diseases and sicknesses, say they of Calvin, who, as Beza writes of him, was much afflicted that way (a). But see even in Epaphroditus, of whom Paul said none was minded like to him, yet he in a good cause was afflicted, and came to great extremities. Seeing then we cannot avoid sickness nor death, but we must all come to it, let us consider briefly how to fit ourselves for it beforehand, that it comes not suddenly, and takes us before we are aware thereof. And herein let us consider what we are to do before sickness, and what in sickness.

(1.) Before sickness labour to make God thy friend, who is Lord of life and death. Is there any hope that a prisoner which abuses the judge continually till he be on the ladder shall have pardon? How can he imagine that a man that all his lifetime followed his own wilful courses of sin, and persecuted, by scandalising and slandering good men; that continually blasphemed God and abused him in his word; how can this man think to command comfort in sickness? How can he think God will be pleased with him? No. All such repentance in sickness may justly be suspected to be hypocritical, that it is made rather for fear of punishment than loathing of sin; and therefore God often leaves such men to despair, and that justly. See what he saith, Prov. 1:25, 'Because I have called, and ye refused; I have stretched out my hand, and no man regarded; I will laugh at your calamity, and mock when your fear cometh,' and so forth to the end of the chapter. It is just with God, seeing when he called you would not answer, that when you call he should not answer. Be wise therefore to foresee the time to come.

(2.) In the second place, if thou wilt be sick to thy comfort, disease not thy soul beforehand. Those that will avoid sickness, they will abstain from such meats and other things as may increase their malady. Let it be thus in our soul sickness; find what thou art sick of, and take heed of hunting after such temptations and occasions as may inflame thy soul. Those that are profane swearers and loose livers they think they shall never hear of their wickedness; they think it will be forgotten and borne withal, whenas, even while they are thus wretched, they distemper both their souls and their own bodies also.

Thus do they eat their own bane. Take away the strength and power of sickness. Take heed of sin beforehand. For it is the sin that thou now committest that breeds sickness. And he that tempts thee now to sin, when sickness comes will tempt thee to despair of pardon.

(3.) Thirdly, Wean thine affections from the earth; for else when any cross comes, we shall not be able to endure. The saying is true, *qui nimis amat, nimis dolet*. In what proportion a man loves this world too much in the enjoyment of it, in that proportion he grieves too much at his departure from it. It is an easy matter for one to die that hath died in heart and affection before. And to help this, consider the uncertainty and vanity of these things, and how unable they will be to help thee when thou shalt stand most in need of help. Men when they are well, they consider not what these things will do, but they consider what they cannot do. Friends in adversity are true friends. Alas, when thou art sick, what will thy friends or thy riches do! Yea, what can they do for thy recovery!

(4.) In the fourth place, make up thy accounts daily, that when sickness and weakness comes we have not our greatest and most laborious work to do. It is an atheistical folly to put off all till sickness, whenas they know not but God may call them by sudden death, or if he warns them by sickness, God may suffer their understanding and senses to be so troubled as they shall neither be able to conceive or judge. Now, what madness is it to put off our hardest works to our weakest estate. There is no day but the best of us gather soil, especially those that have much dealing in the world. We had need to wash ourselves daily, and pray to God that he would cleanse us.

(5.) Fifthly, While thou art in health, lay a foundation and ground of comfort for sickness; and still be doing of something that may further thine account, and testify of the reconciliation between God and thee. It is strange to see how many account of death; send for a minister, be absolved, and take the communion, and say, 'Lord, have mercy on me;' and we presently conclude he is assuredly saved.' Tis true, these are good if well used; but if there be not a foundation laid, these are but miserable comforters. A good death is ever laid in a good life. Absolution to such as these that so lightly esteem of their estate is no other than as a seal to a blank. It is true, we ought to deny absolution to none as will say they repent; but know this, you may be hypocrites, notwithstanding our absolution. We spend all our wits and powers to get unto us a little worldly pelf; and shall we think to go to heaven, and to be carried thither, through pleasures and ease? No. He that made thee without thee will not save thee without thee. This is one reason why we condemn popery; and though we in show hate it, yet are we popish in our conceits. It is the good that in our health we do that comforts us in our sickness; for considering how it hath pleased God not only to put into our minds but into our wills to do this or that good—Such a good man have I raised; such a poor man have I relieved—we think of it as an evidence of God's Spirit in us. Contrarily, when we think how brave our apparel hath been, how gallant our company, what pleasing plays and spectacles we have seen, what can this comfort us? Nay, will it not discomfort us to consider we have spent our means and time unprofitably; we have delighted in worldly delights? How shall I account with that just Judge for my time and means ill spent? Doth not this argue want of grace, want of God's Spirit? Be wise therefore with Joseph against times of famine, of sickness, of death; prepare such cordials as may strengthen thee. Now,

2. In the next place consider we how we are to behave ourselves in sickness.

(1.) First, therefore, know and consider that as Job saith, 'Sickness comes not from the dust,' Job 5:6; but consider thy ways, especially thy antecedent course of life, which of late thou hast passed over next before thy sickness. For God corrects not for sin in general so much as for some one sin that rules. If it appears not, pray to

God to help thee in this thy search: and when thou hast found out the Jonah, the Achan that thus troubleth thee, 'then judge thyself and justify God,' Josh. 7:19.

(2.) 'Judge yourselves, that ye be not judged of the Lord,' 1 Cor. 11:31; lay thyself open by confession; renew thy repentance, and confess thyself thoroughly, and spare not thyself. It is cruelty to be merciful to thyself in this thing. And justify God; say with the holy prophet, 'Just art thou, O Lord, and righteous are thy judgments,' Ps. 119:75; and thus by meeting with God we do allay our sickness. For God uses it no other than as a messenger to call us to meet with him, who else would never look after him; and when the messenger hath his answer, he is gone. When we repent and amend, the sickness departs, unless it be sent for a better end, to call us out of this miserable world, to perfect his promises to us. When therefore God summons thee, do not as the common course is, send first for the bodily physician, and when thou art past natural care,* then for the divine; but contrarily let the divine begin, Ps. 32:3, seq. Until David had confessed his sin, 'his bones waxed old with roaring, and his moisture was turned to the drought of summer.' But when he confessed his sins, 'Thou forgavest the iniquity of my sin;' for indeed the sickness of the body begins from the iniquity of the soul. Begin with it; look to heal it, and comfort in thy bodily estate will follow; and it is just with God to suffer those that trust so to the physician to continue in hope of health, till they be past recovery, and then to send them to their own places, as it was said of Judas, without thinking of their soul's good. Thus, when thou hast found out thy disease, and laid it open to God,

(3.) In the next place, look for evidences of comfort; desire God to witness to thy soul his peace with her; and upon every warning of sickness, look for thy evidence afresh. This will strengthen thee as it did Job. Whatsoever discomforts he saw, 'yet I know my Redeemer liveth, and that I shall see him,' Job 19:25. And thou thus going to God, if thou lookest on the earth, thou wilt count all as dross and dung, as Paul did, Philip. 3:8. All worldly matters will be despised in thine eyes.

(4.) In the fourth place, labour for love. Consider how the world is with us. We know not what will become of us. Begin with justice, in giving every man his own, and then with bounty; then forgive. We cannot go to heaven with anger. Thus did Christ, 'Father, forgive them,' Luke 23:34; and Stephen, 'Lord, lay not this sin to their charge,' Acts 7:60. Be far from revenge. If thou lookest to come where Christ is, do as he did. This is hard to fleshly minds, but it must be done. Thou must first deny thyself before thou canst be saved.

(5.) In the next place, labour for patience; but such as must be ruled by reason, and not blockish. To this end consider, first, whence the sickness is. It is from God who is powerful. [Consider] that we shall get nothing by striving or murmuring; that we cannot resist him so but he will have his will fulfilled upon us; and therefore let us humble ourselves under the mighty hand of God. Then also, consider it comes from God, who is thy Father, and therefore loveth thee. What then though the cup be bitter? Shall I not drink of the cup which my father giveth me to drink of? Know also, that all the circumstances of thy sickness are ordered by him, the degree and time are limited by him, he knows what is needful and fitting, he is Lord of life and death, resign thyself therefore to him; and then hath God his end he looks for, viz., that his children should cast themselves on his mercy. In the next place, remember that thou deservest much worse, and that he shews thee favour in this gentle correction. Remember what Christ hath done for thee, what he hath suffered, what he hath delivered thee from, and what these things are in comparison of those that thou justly deservest.

Consider also what will be the fruit and end of all these thy troubles and griefs, even the quiet fruits of righteousness; all shall be for our good. Is it for thy good rather to drink of a bitter potion than sickness? what though it be bitter? It is for my health; God is working my good. Though I feel it not now, hereafter I shall in his good time. And thus shall we justify God, as David did, and behold him as in Christ a most loving Father who was an angry judge, and being turned, all are turned. Corrections they are now, which were before punishments, and they are become trials of graces.

(6.) In the last place, let us being sick be ever heavenly-minded, thinking on nothing but that which may administer to us spiritual comfort. If we have not this, look not to come thither. It is not fit our minds should be on these earthly things, whenas our souls are going or should be going to heaven. It is God's just judgment to suffer men's minds, being ready to depart the world, to be taken up with the world, and as they have lived, so to die. If we would have a pattern of dying well, look on Christ; before his death, when he was troubled, he will have his disciples with him. So when we are vexed with any temptation or trial, use such company as may bring spiritual comfort to thee, and thereby to strengthen thee. As Christ left his 'peace behind him,' John 14:27, let us study also how to preserve peace after our departure. As Christ did all the good he could so long as he lived, so should we, that our sickness may be fruitful of comfort. As Christ studied how to do all his work, thus should we endeavour to do what we have to do, that with a clear conscience we may say as Christ did, 'Father, I have done the work thou gavest me to do,' John 17:4. Christ had care of his disciples and friends before he died: of his mother, 'Woman, behold this son,' saith he, &c., John 19:26. 'I go away, but I will send you the Comforter,' John 15:26. We also ought to be careful for the well-leaving of them whom God hath committed to our care to provide for. Christ was not vindictive; 'Father, forgive them,' saith he, Luke 23:34. So we, specially when we die in peace, forgive all the world, yea, our enemies, for so also did Stephen. Lastly, Christ commends his soul to God: 'Father, into thy hands I commend my spirit,' saith he, Luke 23:46; dying, he dies in faith and obedience. Thus also ought we to imitate him; die in faith, be sure of God that he is thy Father, and obediently submit thy soul into his hands when thou diest. Thus when we die we shall die with comfort, and we shall count it exceeding joy when we fall into any trouble or adversity whatsoever.

But the Lord

Doct. Observe this comfortable exception: God brings his children low, but he raises them up again, if it be for their good: Ps. 118:17, 'I will not die, but live, and declare the works of the Lord.' Nay, then especially, when they are past all worldly means of recovery; and as it is in sickness, thus also is it in other troubles; and this God doth.

Reason 1. First, To glorify his power the more.

2. Secondly, That his enemies might not triumph still in overcoming us.

3. Thirdly, That we being thus delivered, might consecrate our lives and breath to him anew, as having received them from him, even by a new gift.

Use 1. The use hereof is, If God helps us above and against means, we ought to hope above, yea, against hope, believe in the greatest extremities; 'though he kill us, yet trust in him.' God is not tied to Galen's rules.* He can work above physical moans, as he shewed in the cure of Hezekiah. Especially in soul troubles let not our faith fail us, for he hath absolutely promised his helping hand in them.

Had mercy on him

Observe the language of the Holy Ghost, shewing the recovery of Epaphroditus, by the ground and cause of it, 'God had mercy on him.'

Doct. Observe, therefore, God's mercy is the spring of all God's dealing with us. Both his benefits and his corrections of us all comes from his mercy; all his ways are mercy and truth. We are sick, well; we live, we die; all comes from his mercy. Seeing, therefore, all comes from his mercy, yea, our greatest extremities, because he might have dealt worse with us,

Use 1. Let us look that we wilfully neglect not or cast away mercy, in what estate soever we are.

Doct. In the next place observe, God's mercy extends to this temporal life. We think his mercy is only for things that belong to life everlasting. No. The same love and mercy that gives us heaven, it is the same that gives us our daily bread; and therefore the same faith we must have to God for the things of this life that we have on him for the other life in heaven. And thus did the saints, as we may see in Heb. 11:4, seq.

Use 2. This should direct us not to rest in deliverance, but to look to the ground of it, the mercy of God, and endeavour to taste the love and mercy of God in his gifts, for all his gifts are less than his mercy. This will cause us to have more comfort in our daily bread than the wicked have in all their abundance.

Use 3. Thirdly, We should learn from hence, in giving, to give thy soul and affection; let thy brother have thy heart with thy gifts, and thus shalt thou imitate thy heavenly Father.

Use 4. Lastly, If the very recovery from sickness comes from God's free love and mercy, what can we look for by merit? If health for Epaphroditus his body came from the free mercy of God, how can we expect for to merit the salvation of our souls. No. It must be from God's free grace and mercy in Jesus Christ.

And not on him only, but on me also

As if he had said, It may be for him it had been good to have been taken away, and to have remained with Christ, but God had mercy on me in sparing him.

Obj. But it may be objected, How can it be the mercy of God that spared him, whenas God had rather shewed his mercy in taking him away from the evil to come, and in placing him with himself in glory? and Paul, he desired 'to be dissolved and to be with Christ,' and said it was far better for him so to be.

Ans. I answer, life, and especially health, is God's mercy, for without it life is no life. But why, and how?

1. Because by it we recover our spiritual comfort and assurance of heaven, Ps. 39:13. To this end David

prayed, 'Spare me a little, that I may recover my strength.'

2. Secondly, In regard of others' health, life is a blessing. Thus, Hezekiah desired it, that he might get assurance of his salvation, and praise the Lord, Isa. 38:22.

3. Thirdly, Life is to be desired as a blessing from God, in regard of the church, that we might do good; for after death we are receivers only, and not doers. All the good we convey to others, we must do it while we live here. Therefore it is not unlawful to desire to live to see thy children brought up in the fear of God, and yet let that be with a resignation to God's will and purpose. We see Christ, that had contrary desires, who came to perform his Father's will and to die willingly, yet he said, 'Let this cup pass from me,' Mat. 26:39; for the soul is to be carried to desire as the objects are offered. If thou beest well, rejoice in it, and count it as God's blessing. If thou beest sick, patiently submit thyself to God's will, and count it as his merciful dealing with thee. Indeed, as we look on death being an enemy to our nature, and a destroyer thereof, we desire it not. Yet, considering it as God's decree and will, say still, 'Thy will be done, O Lord, and not mine,' Paul, he considered for himself it was better to die, but looking to the Philippians,

'nevertheless, to abide in the flesh is better for you,' Phil. 1:24. Learn from hence the sweet estate of God's children; whether he lives or dies, all is mercy; and this they have by being assured they have their part in the covenant of grace. Labour therefore to find an interest therein for thyself. Observe, in the next place, God does good to us by others, as here he conveys good to Paul by Epaphroditus his life. Let us therefore praise him for parents, friends, benefactors; for by them God hath mercy on us. God uses man for the good of man, that he might knit the communion of saints together more straightly.* No doubt but the apostle Paul had begged Epaphroditus his life from God, and he here acknowledges it as a great mercy of God. Thus ought we to acknowledge God's mercy on us, by taking mercy on others for our sakes.

VERSE 27

Lest I should have sorrow on sorrow.

Our blessed apostle had sorrowed much for the sickness of Epaphroditus; if he had died, he had had wave on wave. Observe, God's children have not sorrow on sorrow. We have matter of sorrow while we are here, as our corruptions, and the troubles of the church. These minister unto us matter of grief while we are here in this vale of tears. Let us not therefore be delicate nor dainty.

We must sow in tears here, if we would reap hereafter in joy. We must shed tears, if we would hereafter have them wiped away. Yet is the sorrow of a Christian mingled ever with joy to support them. The Lord he weighs and measures the distresses of his children. The rod of the wicked shall not rest upon the godly man's back, Ps. 125:3. And this mingled estate must be till we come into heaven, where all tears shall be wiped away.

Obj. But it will be objected, David had sorrow upon sorrow: one depth calls another, saith he, Ps. 42:7.

Ans. I answer, It is true there may be divers occasions of grief, but God doth so temper them as he giveth joy upon joy, grace upon grace, and comfort upon comfort; faith upon faith, patience upon patience; and it is much better to have access of comfort in extremities than to want extremities and occasions of sorrow, by reason of the good we receive by such trials. And there is no distress but we may gather ground of comfort to ourselves in them. Art thou sick? Bless God that he hath left thee the use of reason and thy wits. Hast thou lost friends, and hath not God taken all away? He leaves thee some, nay, he leaves his Spirit to accompany thee. Paul was in prison, it is true, but did he want comfort? No. God will raise us up with one hand as he casts us down with the other; it is his 'mercy we are not consumed,'

Lam. 3:22. But the wicked they shall have sorrow on sorrow. He lets them ruffle a while here, but at length their judgments come suddenly and unavoidably. He hath no mercy for them if he once begins. Thus did he add judgment to judgment on Pharaoh till he was consumed; and therefore upon little griefs they run into desperate courses, as Cain, Ahithophel. God suffers the wicked to add sin to sin, and so doth he add sorrow to sorrow. Lay up this for our comfort against the ill time. God will not suffer us to be tempted above measure. He will either abate our trouble or enlarge our grace, so as it shall not overwhelm us. Note this example of God as one for us to imitate and to follow. When we see any one afflicted, let us not vex them the more by adding sorrow to sorrow. David he complains of a kind of men that were of the nature of the devil, going over where the wall is lowest, like ill humours that resort all to ill affected places. No. God's children have pitiful and compassionate hearts. Examine therefore thy spirit, whether thou canst weep with them that weep; for as the Spirit of God helps us in misery, so do those that are led by his Spirit. It is the custom, and hath been, of God's children, to comfort those in misery. Thus did Job's friends, although they erred in the performance thereof.

VERSE 28

I sent him therefore more carefully.

In this verse St Paul sets forth the end of sending Epaphroditus, viz., that they might have the more joy, and he the less sorrow. But it will be said, Paul had use of Epaphroditus himself; he was in prison; he had none to comfort him. But it is no wonder for him, that could set light by his own soul for God's people, to part with a friend for the comfort of his people; and this ought we also to respect, namely, the comforts of God's people above all. Thus did this apostle. He was content to forbear the joys of heaven for the good of the Philippians, in the first chapter. The children of God are of excellent spirits. They can overcome and deny themselves.

That when you see him again you may rejoice

The Philippians hereby had a double cause of joy. First, sight of their pastor whom they loved. Seeing friends is more comfortable than all ways of hearing from them; and the joys of heaven are commended to us by the beatifical vision we hear of these joys here. But when we see them, then is our joy accomplished. The second cause of joy was in this, that now they should see Epaphroditus, as given them anew and sent from God; whose love, mercy, goodness, and power is more clearly seen in delivering men from danger than in preserving of men from falling into danger. It is more honour to God, and more comfort to men. For the Philippians received him as a token of God's love to them, and as an effect of their prayers. Let us take notice of the enlargement of God's love to us in delivering and enlarging any of our friends to us free from afflictions.

And I may be the less sorrowful

The apostle was, and we must be sorrowful in this world; but sometimes more, sometimes less. For a Christian's estate is ever full of ebbs and floods. But of this I spake formerly.

VERSE 29

Receive him therefore in the Lord with all gladness.

Our apostle first entreats them generally 'to receive him;' then he shews the manner, 'in the Lord with gladness;' thence he grounds a general, 'make much of such.' But it may be urged—the apostle might have spared this exhortation, for no doubt but the Philippians being glad to see him would receive him. It is true; but this is not all: they must receive him in the Lord,' as a man of God; as a man sent you from God; as a messenger of Christ; and receive him with a holy affection.

Doct. A Christian must do all things in the Lord: marry in the Lord; love in the Lord; salute in the Lord. All matters, both of necessity and courtesy, must be in the Lord. A Christian must 'live in the Lord,' and he must 'die in the Lord.'

Reason. The reason is, for that a Christian in all looks to God. Whatsoever befalls him he receives, whatsoever he does, he does in the Lord, looking only to him, and depending on him. Carnal men contrarily do all things carnally: marries, loves, salutes carnally; he lives carnally, dies carnally. But the Christian's life is ever to die and behold Christ in all things; in all estates; in all his thoughts, words, and deeds; in life, in death. Let this acquaint us with the manner of a Christian's life and estate, and with the language of the Holy Ghost.

And hold such in reputation

Others read it, 'make much of such' (b). The sense is the same with the former. 'Esteem of such as they are;' esteem of such ministers that are faithful as he is; of such Christians as he is; such excellent Christians as he. So as the words have a double reference, as to both his general and particular calling. For his particular calling of the ministry, see how he is formerly commended; that he was painful* and careful, and neglected his own life. Ministers, if they be such, they must be had in repute and esteem. If they be not of the best sort, surely they are of the worst. Angels and good men, none better than the good; none worse than them if they turn. But especially ministers, if they be not good, they are unsavoury as salt;† neither good for the ground, nor yet for the dunghill.

Reason. The reason of this is, for by such as these are God conveys greatest good to men. He builds by them, he plants by them. They are watchmen, husbandmen, they are God's labourers; nay, they are his angels, discovering to the church the secrets of God's counsel. They are as Job saith, but as 'one among a thousand.' Such surely as these are worthy of all respects.

Obj. But it will be objected, they are ever opposite to us, they cross men.

Ans. Even then when they are most opposite they are to be esteemed the more, for they are 'the light of the world.' Their office is to discover the works of darkness. They are husbandmen to break up the fallow grounds of our hearts; and it is our part to embrace them in doing their duties. For it is a note of a wicked man to count such as these troublers. It was Ahab's speech to Elijah, 1 Kings 18:17. God's children loves them and reverences them when they are most sharp; for they know that they themselves do want such reproofs to check their corruptions; they wish their corruptions might be ripped up thoroughly. This is impossible that carnal men should allow of this. They have beloved sins. When they are met with they are touched to the quick, no marvel therefore if they repine. A true Christian will acknowledge and esteem the meanest part of them blessed and beautiful. The carnal man may esteem ministers indeed, but such as cry 'Peace, peace, when there is no peace,' Jer. 6:14; and surely such a prophet is a fit prophet for such a people. But let the true Christian love and reverence those that are the messengers of peace, and esteem of them by so much the more, by how much their degree in grace is the greater; for there will he an affection suitable to the proportion of grace they have.

And to this end observe with me some motives to incite us to this duty; and first, 1. It is the character of the child of God, and a sign we are translated from death to life, if we love and reverence the brethren. If we be brethren as we profess ourselves, we are led with the same spirit; and therefore we ought to love those most especial that are means of begetting the grace of the Spirit in us. It is a part of grace to desire grace. Now there is no desire of grace but there must be a love of it; and therefore if we will prove ourselves to be marked with the mark of God in our foreheads, and that we are his children, let us get this character for a witness to us.

2. The second motive in regard of God,—the former was in regard of ourselves,—those that God esteems most we ought to make most account of. God spared not his own Son for their sake. The saints are precious in the eyes of the Lord. And in the second place, Christ he esteems of them above his own blood; he gave himself for them freely. Thirdly, the angels they esteem of them. Christ says, Offend them not, for the angels in heaven behold the face of God continually, Mat. 18:10. Fourthly, the ministers esteem them. 'I suffer all for the elect's sake,' says Paul. The Spirit of God esteems them; they are his temples to dwell in, 2 Tim. 2:10.

3. In regard of themselves they are to be esteemed, they are lively. They have the 'new creature' in them; they have God's Spirit ever in them. All created excellency is as 'the flower of grass.' It withers suddenly. But they have that which continues for ever, grace and the Spirit of God. They have the image of God seated in them. They have the word and the promises made sure to them. They are free-born; free from hell, death, wrath. They are of disposition free; they can want and they can abound. They are rich in the best riches, strong in the greatest strength. They overcome the devil, the world; they overcome and conquer death, who is the king of fears.

4. In the next place, in regard of the good we reap by them they are to be esteemed. God blesses us by them. They are the pillars of this tottering world. In regard of a few of God's elect not yet brought in, this world continues yet; but if the number be accomplished once, God will no longer withhold his coming. Lot's presence in Sodom stayed God's wrath; he could do nothing till he was gone. So Noah in the old world, Joseph in Egypt, Moses among the Israelites, they stopped the passage of God's wrath; and therefore Job, 22:30, saith, 'He shall deliver the island of the innocent.' They are 'the chariots and horsemen of Israel;' their prayers are our protectors. And thus mayest thou try thyself and thy estate; for dost thou despise those that are good, thou art ranked amongst vile persons. Look 2 Tim. 3:3, and such as are signs of the last times, wherein corruption shall abound. Many things are much set by, but where are those that have their delight set on the excellent of the earth? A wicked man, I deny not, may esteem some one that is good, but it shall not be for that they are good, but it may be for some by-respects of profit or pleasure that they shall reap thereby. They will commend stars that be within their own horizon; praise martyrs being dead, whom, if alive, likely it is they would be the first persecutors of them; for thirty pieces of silver, a little gain, sell even Christ himself, and make shipwreck of their faith. Yet the time will shortly come when these despised shall be had in

greatest honour, and those that scorn them now would be glad to keep them company, and ever be with them.

Quest. But it will be asked, Where are these men you speak of? how is it they are not respected?

Ans. I answer, They are not known, 'the world knows them not;'—First, Because it knows not their Father; for if it esteemed him, it would esteem also of them; and therefore, Secondly, they are 'strangers and pilgrims,' although excellent in themselves. Thirdly, 'Their life is hid with Christ,' Col. 3:3. They are eclipsed and disgraced. Disgraces, scandals, miseries, and their own infirmities, these make the children of God to be unknown; yet those that know them will even in their infirmities see many things worth observation and practice. Contrarily in wicked men what is to be respected? Shall we think of them the better for their degree, state, comeliness, riches, or the like? Surely these end in death, whenas all respects are taken away; but goodness is more accomplished in death, it shall never be at an end; and therefore to be the rather respected and esteemed, and men also as they are good. Wicked men may be also esteemed, but not otherwise than as they are marked with the image of God, as they are in place of magistracy and government; and so they are not esteemed, but their images they carry about with them of superiority. And therefore among these of the like kind those are to be most esteemed that are most good, and this is, as I said before, a note of a good man; for what saith David, Ps. 15:4? 'He shall enter into the tabernacle of God, in whose eyes a vile person is contemned; but he honoureth them that fear the Lord.' To this end begin with thyself. How dost thou value thyself? Dost thou do it carnally? How then canst thou esteem aright of others? Be therefore of Theodosius his mind, 'value thyself according to thy measure in grace and assurance of salvation' (c). What though the world think basely of thee! So did it of those saints, Heb. 11:38. They thought them unworthy to live. But remember God is not ashamed to be called our God and Father. Heaven is ours, Christ, grace, and glory are all ours. Thus by esteeming thyself aright thou shalt begin to reverence that in others which thou so much accountest of in thyself; and we all together shall find what God esteems most of, and of whom, when we shall be together crowned with joys unspeakable, which are hidden from the eyes of the world. It appears not to them what we shall be, the glory being such and so great as they, judging carnally, cannot conceive thereof.

VERSE 30

Because for the work of Christ he was nigh to death.

This work of Christ especially aims at works of mercy to Paul while he was in prison, and for these he is said to be nigh to death. By his long and tedious journey he took a sickness, and thereby was nigh to death. And these are called 'the works of Christ;' partly because all good works are from Christ—for he commands them, he allows them, he did them—and partly also because in the doing of them our aim is at Christ's honour. So then the excellency of good works consists not in doing those which are good in their own nature, but in well doing of them. All our particular actions must be done with having an eye on and a respect to Christ. What if therefore thou doest any good thing with an eye on credit or a good name, nay, if of mere pity, without respect of Christ's command, example, and obedience thereunto; all that thou doest in this manner cannot merit the name of a good work, or a work of Christ. For Christ saith, that which you do to any of his little ones you do to him. And do you think that he will take it done to him, when he seeth in thy heart that thou regardest by-respects, and never intendest him in the thing thou doest? No. You did it for commendation, to get popular applause, or for your own profit, or the like. Let it not be with us in this manner. Let us do all things commanded in the second table, as in obedience of the first, to glorify God. Let us do good works thoroughly, though they cost us labour, cost, and danger; also pray zealously, give cheerfully.

'Cursed is he that doth the work of the Lord negligently,' Jer. 48:10. Give freely therefore to every one in whom Christ comes a-begging to thee. 'This is pure religion before God and undefiled, to visit the fatherless and widows,' James 1:27; but see that you keep yourselves 'unspotted of the world.' And these things done as they ought to be, will comfort us on our deathbed, and be an assurance to our consciences of our faith, and will strengthen us when all other works, done for any self-respect, shall be so far from comforting us, as they shall weaken and discomfort us, and bear witness to our guilty consciences of our hypocrisy. But to proceed. It may seem St Paul was ill advised of his work of Epaphroditus, that he called it a work of Christ, when it had like to have cost him his life. Yet ought it not to seem strange, for by this very pattern we learn not to avoid or fly from the doing of any work of Christ; no, though by doing of it we incur danger of our lives. For the best good must take the chief and first place with us; and by how much the soul is more excellent than the body, by so much is the good of the soul to be preferred before the good of the body. He that hates not father, mother, yea, his own life, in respect of God's glory, cannot be the disciple of Christ. God would have us exercise our judgments in these things beforehand, that we may go about all such things with a holy and zealous resolution. Hence we may gather grounds to answer divers doubts.

1st Quest. As, first, whether in time of persecution we ought to lose our lives or deny the truth?

Ans. To this I answer, out of the example of Epaphroditus, affirmatively, that we ought rather to lose our lives than deny the truth; for God's truth is better than our lives. It was commendable in Priscilla and Aquila that they laid down their necks for Paul's life, Rom. 16:3, 4; much more is the truth of God's word to be esteemed above man's life. And they are counted wise that have that esteem; as the martyrs, whose estate is accounted a blessed estate.

2d Quest. Furthermore, it will be asked, Whether a minister ought to leave his congregation in the time of pestilence, or not?

Ans. I answer, upon the same ground, he ought not; for he is not, in regard of the work of God, to esteem his own life. But so as he is not bound to a particular visitation of every one whom it hath pleased God to visit with sickness, neither ought the sick party to require this at the hands of the pastor; but rather to reserve him to the general good of all of them, and the rather to spare him. Thus did Beza. And in the law the leprous person was to go about and to cry 'Unclean, unclean,' to the end that others might not unawares be polluted by him. And therefore every one ought to be a good husband for himself, to lay up with himself grounds of comfort against such a time as it may please God to afflict him in any such manner. Another question may hence be answered.

3d Quest. Whether a man may equivocate to save his own life?

Ans. I answer: If a man be lawfully called to answer for himself, he must know that he ought to tell the truth, and not to be ashamed thereof; for why do men live but to live honestly, and to keep a good conscience? And it is more necessary that truth should flourish and be cleared than that thou shouldst live. Those that now are ashamed to confess the truth, the God of truth will be ashamed of them hereafter. And therefore a fourth question may arise.

4th Quest. Whether a man may break prison to save himself?

Ans. I answer: Thou oughtest not to do anything that may endanger another man to save thine own life; and therefore mayest not, by breaking of prison, endanger the jailor's life to save thyself. And the reasons are, for that it shames the truth and equity of thy cause; and therefore when the prison doors were open Paul would not fly, Acts 16:28, seq. Peter did it indeed, he came out of prison; but it was an extraordinary and miraculous deliverance by the command of the angel, Acts 12:11. Secondly, it is a contempt of magistracy and law; for every man is to be governed by and to submit himself to the law.

5th Quest. Again, some have doubted whether a minister, being called to a place of unwholesome air, whether he may leave it.

Ans. I answer: Let them consider before they go whether they shall be able to endure or not; but if they be once called, and are there, let them look to the salvation of God's people, and provide for themselves as they may. We see Epaphroditus neglects his own life for the service of God.

6th Quest. A sixth question or doubt may hence be resolved, Whether, in case of persecution, a minister may fly.

Ans. I answer: We may fly for our own safeties; and a minister may, if there be those left that being good shepherds will stand for the flock, that it be not scattered. Yet if God gives thee a spirit of courage to hold out, consult thou with God by earnest prayer for the direction of his Holy Spirit, and he will assuredly direct thee; for if out of thine own confidence thou shouldst stand out, and afterward give back, it would weaken and discourage others, who else it may be would stand out. Yet if thou beest once taken, whether thou art a minister or not, thou art under the law, thou must obey.

7th Quest. And in the seventh place, we may and ought to be ready to lay down our lives for the commonwealth, for common good is to be preferred before private good. The hand doth endanger itself for the good of the head, and therefore a private man may venture himself to save a public person; and from hence is grounded the lawfulness of a Christian war.

Quest. But it will be asked, How shall we come to this resolution, to lay down our lives for the truth?

Ans. I answer: First, thou must labour to have thy judgment enlightened, discern of the order of good things; and this only a Christian can get to account of his life but slightly in comparison, knowing that it is 'but a vapour that soon vanisheth,' James 4:14, and that the peace of conscience will never leave a man till it hath brought him to eternity. He knows also the terrors of conscience are above all terrors, and that it will never leave him. He knows the world cannot be worth a soul, that nothing can redeem it being once lost; and these things being truly learned, we shall be ready to deny father, mother, yea, our very life, if they once oppose

Christ; and thus shall we beforehand get a resolution by daily considering these things, and a mind truly prepared for all trials. And to that end put cases with thyself. Now, what thou wouldst do or suffer rather than be drawn to offend God, if the time of trial were now to come. If thy heart doth tell thee that thou canst forego all, and countest them as nought in respect of Christ, surely God he accepts of this thy resolution. If thou canst not find this in thee, know for a certainty thy faith is but weak. And therefore consider with thyself, that if thou come to this, to lose all for Christ, thou shalt be no loser. The peace of conscience is above all good that can be desired; and [consider] that thy life is not thine own, for both it, our estate, friends, are all of God's gift to us, who may take them when he will. But if they be lost for God's service, thou shalt be no loser. It cannot stand with God's justice to suffer it. Let this bring shame upon many that will do nothing for the church, lose no credit amongst the wicked men, part with no jot of their goods, take no pains nor labour. We see it that martyrs they will spend their blood. Esther counted not her life dear unto her: 'If I perish, I perish,' 4:16. And yet these are loath to venture displeasure of some inferior, mean person. How can such ever think to get assurance of salvation? In this case those that thus love their lives do hate them, and that which they fear shall fall suddenly on them; as it was with those that, starting aside for fear, and denying their profession, thinking to save themselves from the fire, they fell into a worse fire, the hell of a guilty conscience, which cannot be quenched, nor they made insensible thereof.

Richard Sibbes

Richard Sibbes (1577-1635),

Richard Sibbes (1577-1635), one of the most influential figures in the Puritan movement during the earlier years of the seventeenth century. He was renowned for the rich quality of his ministry. **The Providence Of God** is a book by Richard Sibbes that comforts the despondent and fearful Christian using the words of Matthew 12:20 (which quotes Isaiah), "A bruised reed he will not break, and a smoldering wick he will not snuff out." Many Christians have found this book to be remedy to doubt and burden.

.

Review

'I shall never cease to be grateful to...Richard Sibbes who was balm to my soul at a period in my life when I was overworked and badly overtired, and therefore subject in an unusual manner to the onslaughts of the devil...I found at that time that Richard Sibbes, who was known in London in the early seventeenth century as "The Heavenly Doctor Sibbes" was an unfailing remedy... **The Providence Of God**.. quieted, soothed, comforted, encouraged and healed me.' --*D. Martyn Lloyd-Jones*

Richard Sibbes

Pathways To The Past

Each volume stands alone as an Individual Book
Each volume stands together with others
to enhance the value of your collection

Build your Personal, Pastoral or Church Library
Pathways To The Past contains an ever-expanding list of
Christendom's most influential authors

Augustine of Hippo

Athanasius

E. M. Bounds

John Bunyan

Robert Lewis Darby

Brother Lawrence

Jessie Penn-Lewis

Bernard of Clairvaux

Andrew Murray

Watchman Nee

Arthur W. Pink

Thomas Watson

Hannah Whitall Smith

R. A. Torrey

A. W. Tozer

Jean-Pierre de Caussade

And many, many more.

Richard Sibbes

Richard Sibbes

www.ingramcontent.com/pod-product-compliance
Lightning Source LLC
Chambersburg PA
CBHW050334120526
44592CB00014B/2182